Algrove Publishing Limited
36 Mill Street, P.O. Box 1238
Almonte, Ontario, Canada K0A 1A0

Telephone: (613) 256-0350
Fax: (613) 256-0360
Email: sales@algrove.com

Library and Archives Canada Cataloguing in Publication

Williams, J. R. (James Robert), 1888-1957
    Classic cowboy cartoons : from his "Out our way" series / J.R. Williams.

(Classic reprint series)
ISBN 1-897030-15-0 (v.1)

      1. American wit and humor, Pictorial. 2. Cowboys--Caricatures and cartoons. I. Title.
II. Series: Classic reprint series (Almonte, Ont.)

NC1429.W573A4 2004c   741.5'973   C2004-904421-4

Printed in Canada
#1-8-04

Publisher's Note

James Robert Williams was born in Nova Scotia in 1888 and his family moved to Detroit before he started school. At age 15 he quit school to apprentice as a machinist, moving to Arkansas and then Oklahoma where he spent six years drifting around the territory working as a cowboy on different ranches before spending three years in the U.S. Cavalry. After he married, he took a full-time job with a crane company in Ohio. He started cartooning professionally in 1922 with the daily cartoon "Out Our Way", drawing heavily on his experiences in the military, in machine shops and on ranches. At the peak of his career "Out Our Way" was carried by some 700 newspapers. He bought his own ranch in 1930 and continued drawing until his death in 1957. His lifetime production was in excess of 10,000 cartoons.

Leonard G. Lee, Publisher
Almonte, Ontario
August 2004

How We Make Our Books - *You may not have noticed, but this book is quite different from other softcover books you might own. The vast majority of paperbacks, whether mass-market or the more expensive trade paperbacks, have the pages sheared and notched at the spine so that they may be glued together. The paper itself is often of newsprint quality. Over time, the paper will brown and the spine will crack if flexed. Eventually the pages fall out.*

All of our softcover books, like our hardcover books, have sewn bindings. The pages are sewn in signatures of sixteen or thirty-two pages and these signatures are then sewn to each other. They are also glued at the back but the glue is used primarily to hold the cover on, not to hold the pages together.

We also use only acid-free paper in our books. This paper does not yellow over time. A century from now, this book will have paper of its original color and an intact binding, unless it has been exposed to fire, water, or other catastrophe.

There is one more thing you will note about this book as you read it; it opens easily and does not require constant hand pressure to keep it open. In all but the smallest sizes, all our books will also lie open on a table, something that a book bound only with glue will never do unless you have broken its spine.

The cost of these extras is well below their value and while we do not expect a medal for incorporating them, we did want you to notice them.

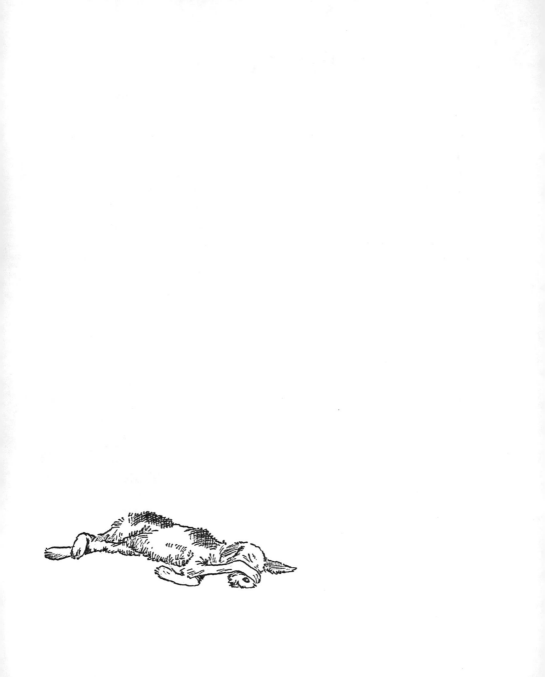

Classic Cowboy Cartoons
Vol. I

J.R.WILLIAMS

Algrove Publishing
Classic Reprint Series

Curly

Curly can be called the 'star' of the strip. He's a traditional cowboy with a big heart that extends to every living thing on the ranch, man and beast alike.

Wes

Wes is a young tender-foot from the east and the ranch bookkeeper. He's learning the ropes but often ends up wound up in them.

Stiffy

Stiffy is an old hand who once worked with Will Rogers. He has cowboyed in Argentina, Canada and nearly every cattle state in the Union. He's set in his ways.

Cooky

Cooky is the camp cook whose temper can be as bad as his grub. Although he and his cuisine are the brunt of many jokes, he can dish out as good as he gets. With a spatula in one hand and a pipe in the other, he doesn't take any guff.

Cotton

You will see the wonderful expressions of Cotton in almost all of the frames but rarely will you see him addressed by his name.

Smokey

Smokey is another bunk-mate that you will see in almost every situation. He is rarely referred to by name but he's the object of attention in a few frames.

THE ONE MAN FLAPPER.

HEROES ARE MADE—NOT BORN.   J.R.WiLLiAMS

SQUATTERS RIGHTS

J.P.WILLIAMS

3

THE RUN DOWN CAKE O' SOAP.

4

THE GAS PIPE.

J.P.WILLIAMS

THE TIE THAT BINDS.

J.R.WILLIAMS

7

WE CONCEDE A ROOTIN' HOG'S NOSE
IS MADE FER YEARS O' WEAR,
AN' TH' CORDED TIRES ON AUTO'S
IS MADE FER MILES O' TEAR.
OUR COOK KIN FORGE A FLAP JACK
WHUT WEARS YORE TEETH OFF FLAT.
BUT TH' THING HAINT YET INVENTED
TOUGHER THAN A COWBOY'S HAT.

J.P.WILLIAMS

8

9

THE RUBBERNECK.

J.R.WILLIAMS

THE JUGGLER.

THE DISTURBING ELEMENT.

J.R.WILLIAMS

12

SAFETY ZONES.

THE MIDNIGHT LUNCH.

J.P.WILLIAMS

GRATITUDE.

J.P.WILLIAMS

UP ON HIS TOES.

PANTS PRESSED WHILE YOU WEIGHT.

J.R.WILLIAMS

17

A CHIP OFF THE OL' BLOCK.

J.R.WILLIAMS

CUTTING REMARKS.

J.P.WILLIAMS

TUNING OUT AN OLD ONE.

J.P.WILLIAMS

THE BARBECUE.

23

LOST IDENTITY.

ARTISTIC TEMPERAMENT

J.P.WILLIAMS

THE ORCHID AND THE CACTUS

J.R.WILLIAMS

THE DISCOVERY OF GENIUS.

27

FOOT NOTES.

THE ROUND UP.

THE STIRRUP WALTZ.

TURN ABOUT.

THE MODERNIST.

J.P.WILLIAMS

HEROES ARE MADE – NOT BORN.

J.R.WILLIAMS

A FORCED LANDING.

J.R.WILLIAMS

LATE LUNCH.

A BAD CONNECTION.

J.P.WILLIAMS

THE BOUNDER

J.R.WILLIAMS

HEROES ARE MADE — NOT BORN.

BOOTS

WE'VE HEARD FOLKS OFFEN ASKIN'
WHY COWBOYS ALL WEAR BOOTS,
BUT IT SEEMS A BIT LIKE ASKIN'
WHY BALLOONS HAVE PARACHUTES.
MEN WHO PUT THER FOOT IN TROUBLE
EVERY DAY 'ER JUST ABOUT,
ER BOUND T'SEE A MOMENT
WHEN THEY WANT T'GIT IT OUT.

J.R.WiLLiAMS

CREASED.

J.P.WILLIAMS

41

HEROES ARE MADE~NOT BORN.

J.R.WILLIAMS

A HOT SKETCH

J.P.WILLIAMS

EAR MARKS.

J.R.WiLLiaMS

A BURNING DESIRE.

J.P.WILLIAMS

47

PAY DAY
JUST A DEAR LITTLE SHACK
WITH A WINDOW ON TH' BACK.

APRIL FOOL?

49

THE AVALANCHE.

FLAT TIRES.

J.P.WILLIAMS

COAT OF ARMS

J.P.WiLLIAMS

52

THE TELEGRAM
(HIS MOTHER)

J.R.WILLIAMS

53

THE COWBOY AND THE CALVES.

THE TALLY

J.P. WILLIAMS

55

HIS NAME HAINT ON NO TABLETS,
IN NO PARK HIS STATUE STANDS.
ALL HIS LIFE HE GRUBBED FER WAGES
YUH COULD TELL IT BY HIS HANDS,
TH' WEALTH HE LEFT BEHIND 'IM
WOULDN'T LOAD A SARDINE CAN,
BUT I'D LIKE T' GOT T' THANK 'IM
FER JES BEIN' MY OL' MAN.

J.R.WiLLiAMS

"DOGS" SENSE.

THE RANGE FINDER.

J.P.WILLIAMS

HEROES ARE MADE - NOT BORN.

MIND AND MATTER.

"WHERE MEN ARE MEN".

61

BUMP READING.

PIE PANNING.

J.R.WILLIAMS

SENSITIVENESS

J.P.WILLIAMS

(Y)EAR MARKS.

J.R.WILLIAMS

THE GREAT DIVIDE.

J.P.WILLIAMS

CATTY.

J.P.WILLIAMS

THE NEW OUT~FIT.

J.P.WILLIAMS

THE RUSTLERS.

FALLING BEHIND IN HIS WORK.

LATE LUNCH.

J.P.WILLIAMS

HEROES ARE MADE—NOT BORN.

74

THE COMMUNITY LOOP.

J.R.WILLIAMS

75

A NO-HIT GAME.

DONE.

J.P.WILLIAMS

SIMILARITY BREEDS COMMENT.

HEROES ARE MADE — NOT BORN.

A BOUNCING BABY.

THE LITERARY HOUR

J.R.WILLIAMS

THE BROKEN SILENCE.

J.R.WILLIAMS

HEROES ARE MADE — NOT BORN.

A TEN YEAR SENTENCE.

85

SPRINGIN A NEW ONE.

J.R.WILLIAMS

THE FIVE FOOT SHELF OF CLASSICS.

THE MAGIC CARPET.

MOMENTS WE'D LIKE TO LIVE OVER.

PASTURE IZED

J.R.WiLLiAMS

THE VICTUAL VIGILANTES.

J.P.WILLIAMS

THE BOARD OF HEALTH.

NOT TO THE VICTOR BELONGS THE SPOILTS.

PILING UP A LEAD.

J.R.WILLIAMS

THE MOST BEAUTIFUL FACE I'VE LOOKED INTO~
A FACE YUH COULD GAZE AT ALL DAY,
IN SUMMER BROKE OUT WITH SOME PIMPLES'
THET TOOK ALL ITS BEAUTY AWAY.

J.R.WILLIAMS

"THEM AS HAS GITS"

J.P.WiLLiAMS

THE DUDE WRANGLER

J.P.WILLIAMS

A TOUCH OF TENDERNESS.

J.P.WILLIAMS

A HINT TO THE WISE.

J.R.WILLIAMS

BLIND ALLEYS.

PILLS.

"MEMORIES OF FRANCE."

WHEN AN IMMOVABLE BODY MEETS AN IMMOVABLE BODY

J. R. WILLIAMS

GOOD FOR MAN OR BEAST.

YOUTH.

THE BACK TO NATURE MOVEMENT.

J.P.WILLIAMS

THE HOLLOW DAY.

110

THE HARPOON THROWER.

J.P.WILLIAMS

THE LOOK IN.

J.P.WILLIAMS

112

NON-SKID TREAD.

BRINGING OUT THE OLD.

J.R.WILLIAMS

NEWS PAPER CIRCULATION.   J.R.WILLIAMS

STRIKING IMPRESSIONS.

J.R.WILLIAMS

STRAINED RELATIONS.

118

THE STRAIGHT AND NARROW.   J.R.WILLIAMS

HEROES ARE MADE~NOT BORN.

J.P. WILLIAMS

THE BOOT JACK.

"READY FOR TH' RIVER"

J.R.WILLIAMS

124

WHEN WHAT COMES UP WON'T GO DOWN

HEROES ARE MADE~NOT BORN.

PORK AND BEANED.

J.P.WILLIAMS

THE FALSE FINDERS.

J.R.WILLIAMS

HEROES ARE MADE — NOT BORN.

J.R.WILLIAMS

FAS TIN'

THE COW COUNTRY.

HENS AND WORMS.

HEROES ARE MADE - NOT BORN.

THE CUPIDS

OPPORTUNITY AT THE DOOR

J.R.WILLIAMS

THE HARD BOILED AIG.

J.R.WILLIAMS

WAR CLOUDS

J.P.WILLIAMS

COW GOILS.

BACHELOR BUTT INS

J.R.WiLLIAMS

THE DOG BLANKETS.

THE SHOCK ABSORBERS.

J.R.WILLIAMS

If you are a fan of J.R. Williams, you may be
interested in our other Williams Classic Reprints.

The Bull of the Woods

U.S. Cavalry Cartoons

Publications by Algrove Publishing Limited

The following is a list of titles from our popular "*Classic Reprint Series*" as well as a list of other publications by *Algrove Publishing Limited.*

Classic Reprint Series

Item #	Title
49L8093	☐ 507 MECHANICAL MOVEMENTS
49L8024	☐ 1800 MECHANICAL MOVEMENTS AND DEVICES
49L8055	☐ 970 MECHANICAL APPLIANCES AND NOVELTIES OF CONSTRUCTION
49L8038	☐ A BOOK OF ALPHABETS WITH PLAIN, ORNAMENTAL, ANCIENT AND MEDIAEVAL STYLES
49L8096	☐ A GLOSSARY OF TERMS USED IN ENGLISH ARCHITECTURE
49L8074	☐ ARE YOU A GENIUS? WHAT IS YOUR I.Q?
49L8101	☐ ARTS-CRAFTS LAMPS & SHADES – *HOW TO MAKE THEM*
49L8016	☐ BARN PLANS & OUTBUILDINGS
49L8046	☐ BEAUTIFYING THE HOME GROUNDS
49L8090	☐ BOAT-BUILDING AND BOATING
49L8014	☐ BOOK OF TRADES
49L8004	☐ BOULTON & PAUL, LTD. 1898 CATALOGUE
49L8012	☐ BOY CRAFT
49L8077	☐ CAMP COOKERY
49L8082	☐ CANADIAN WILD FLOWERS
49L8098	☐ CATALOG OF MISSION FURNITURE 1913 – *COME-PACKT FURNITURE*
49L8106	☐ CLASSIC COWBOY CARTOONS VOL. I
49L8072	☐ CLASSIC PUZZLES AND HOW TO SOLVE THEM
49L8048	☐ CLAY MODELLING AND PLASTER CASTING
49L8005	☐ COLONIAL FURNITURE
49L8065	☐ COPING SAW WORK
49L8032	☐ DECORATIVE CARVING, PYROGRAPHY AND FLEMISH CARVING
49L8092	☐ DETAIL, COTTAGE AND CONSTRUCTIVE ARCHITECTURE
49L8086	☐ FARM BLACKSMITHING
49L8031	☐ FARM MECHANICS
49L8029	☐ FARM WEEDS OF CANADA
49L8015	☐ FENCES, GATES & BRIDGES
49L8056	☐ FLORA'S LEXICON
49L8087	☐ FORGING
49L8706	☐ FROM LOG TO LOG HOUSE
49L8091	☐ FURNITURE DESIGNING AND DRAUGHTING
49L8103	☐ GRANDMOTHER'S PUZZLE BOOK
49L8049	☐ HANDBOOK OF TURNING
49L8027	☐ HANDY FARM DEVICES AND HOW TO MAKE THEM
49L0720	☐ HOMES & INTERIORS OF THE 1920'S
49L8002	☐ HOW TO PAINT SIGNS & SHO' CARDS
49L8054	☐ HOW TO USE THE STEEL SQUARE
49L8001	☐ LEE'S PRICELESS RECIPES
49L8078	☐ MANUAL OF SEAMANSHIP FOR BOYS AND SEAMEN OF THE ROYAL NAVY, 1904
49L8097	☐ MASSEY-HARRIS CIRCA 1914 CATALOG
49L8020	☐ MISSION FURNITURE, HOW TO MAKE IT
49L8081	☐ MR. PUNCH WITH ROD AND GUN – *THE HUMOUR OF FISHING AND SHOOTING*
49L8073	☐ NAME IT! THE PICTORIAL QUIZ BOOK
49L8033	☐ ORNAMENTAL AND DECORATIVE WOOD CARVINGS
49L8089	☐ OVERSHOT WATER WHEELS FOR SMALL STREAMS

Item #	Title
49L8059	☐ PROJECTS FOR WOODWORK TRAINING
49L8705	☐ REFLECTIONS ON THE FUNGALOIDS
49L8003	☐ RUSTIC CARPENTRY
49L8095	☐ SAILING SHIPS AT A GLANCE
49L8044	☐ SAM LOYD'S PICTURE PUZZLES
49L8030	☐ SHELTERS, SHACKS & SHANTIES
49L8085	☐ SKELETON LEAVES AND PHANTOM FLOWERS
49L8068	☐ SPECIALIZED JOINERY
49L8052	☐ STANLEY COMBINATION PLANES – *THE 45, THE 50 & THE 55*
49L8050	☐ STRONG'S BOOK OF DESIGNS
49L8064	☐ THE ARCHITECTURE OF COUNTRY HOUSES
49L8034	☐ THE ART OF WHITTLING
49L8018	☐ THE BOY'S BOOK OF MECHANICAL MODELS
49L8071	☐ THE BULL OF THE WOODS, VOL. 1
49L8080	☐ THE BULL OF THE WOODS, VOL. 2
49L8104	☐ THE BULL OF THE WOODS, VOL. 3
45L0106	☐ THE DUCHESS OF BLOOMSBURY STREET
49L8021	☐ THE INTERNATIONAL CYCLOPEDIA OF MONOGRAMS
49L8053	☐ THE METALWORKING LATHE
49L8023	☐ THE OPEN TIMBER ROOFS OF THE MIDDLE AGES
49L8099	☐ THE SAILOR'S WORD-BOOK
49L8076	☐ THE WILDFLOWERS OF AMERICA
49L8057	☐ THE WILDFLOWERS OF CANADA
49L8058	☐ THE YANKEE WHALER
49L8094	☐ THE YOUNG MILL-WRIGHT AND MILLER'S GUIDE
49L8025	☐ THE YOUNG SEA OFFICER'S SHEET ANCHOR
49L8047	☐ TIMBER – *FROM THE FOREST, TO ITS USE IN COMMERCE*
49L8061	☐ TRADITIONS OF THE NAVY
49L8042	☐ TURNING FOR AMATEURS
49L8107	☐ U.S. CAVALRY CARTOONS
49L8039	☐ VIOLIN MAKING AS IT WAS, AND IS
49L8079	☐ WILLIAM BULLOCK & CO. – *HARDWARE CATALOG, CIRCA 1850*
49L8019	☐ WINDMILLS AND WIND MOTORS
49L8013	☐ YOU CAN MAKE IT
49L8035	☐ YOU CAN MAKE IT FOR CAMP & COTTAGE
49L8036	☐ YOU CAN MAKE IT FOR PROFIT

Other Algrove Publications

Item #	Title
49L8601	☐ ALL THE KNOTS YOU NEED (HARD COVER)
49L8602	☐ ALL THE KNOTS YOU NEED (SOFT COVER)
49L8707	☐ BUILDING THE NORWEGIAN SAILING PRAM (MANUAL AND PLANS)
49L8708	☐ BUILDING THE SEA URCHIN (MANUAL AND PLANS)
49L8084	☐ THE ART OF ARTHUR WATTS
49L8067	☐ WOOD HANDBOOK – *WOOD AS AN ENGINEERING MATERIAL*
49L8060	☐ WOODEN PLANES AND HOW TO MAKE THEM

Algrove Publishing Limited
36 Mill Street, P.O. Box 1238, Almonte, Ontario, Canada K0A 1A0
Telephone: (613) 256-0350 Fax: (613) 256-0360 Email: sales@algrove.com